Starlight & Stone

A mindfulness colouring book inspired by Iona

Emma Major

Copyright © Emma Major 2024

First published 2024 by
Wild Goose Publications
Suite 9, Fairfield
1048 Govan Road, Glasgow G51 4XS, Scotland
A division of Iona Community Trading CIC
Limited Company Reg. No. SC156678
www.ionabooks.com

ISBN 978-1-80432-345-8

All rights reserved. No part of this publication may be reproduced in any form or by any means, including photocopying or any information storage or retrieval system, without written permission from the publisher via PLSclear.com.

Emma Major has asserted her right in accordance with the Copyright, Designs and Patents Act, 1988, to be identified as the author of this work.

Overseas distribution
Australia: Willow Connection Pty Ltd, 1/13 Kell Mather Drive, Lennox Head NSW 2478
New Zealand: Pleroma, Higginson Street, Otane 4170, Central Hawkes Bay

Printed by Bell & Bain, Thornliebank, Glasgow

With your pencils and crayons in hand, embark on a mindful pilgrimage of colour through these images inspired by Iona.

Forget walking shoes, a compass and dusty maps of faraway lands; this pilgrimage can be followed every day, in a mindful way, with just your coloured pencils or crayons in hand.

Creativity is within us all, just waiting to be released and bring peace in the busy everyday. By colouring these images you allow your mind to quieten whilst your hands are busy, finding a place of peace and stillness at any time.

Unwind and connect with the spirit of Iona as you illuminate intricate stars and timeless Celtic crosses, losing yourself in the small details and soothing patterns.

By the end of the book, you'll have a renewed appreciation for your coloured pencils and a collection of artwork that reflects your creative journey. Remember, there's no right or wrong way to colour – just relax, explore, and have fun!

Creativity is my sanity
Cathartically speaking, it's my therapy
The place I face my emotions
Work through worries and concerns
Expressing myself in lines and colour
It's healing in a way like no other
-Emma Major

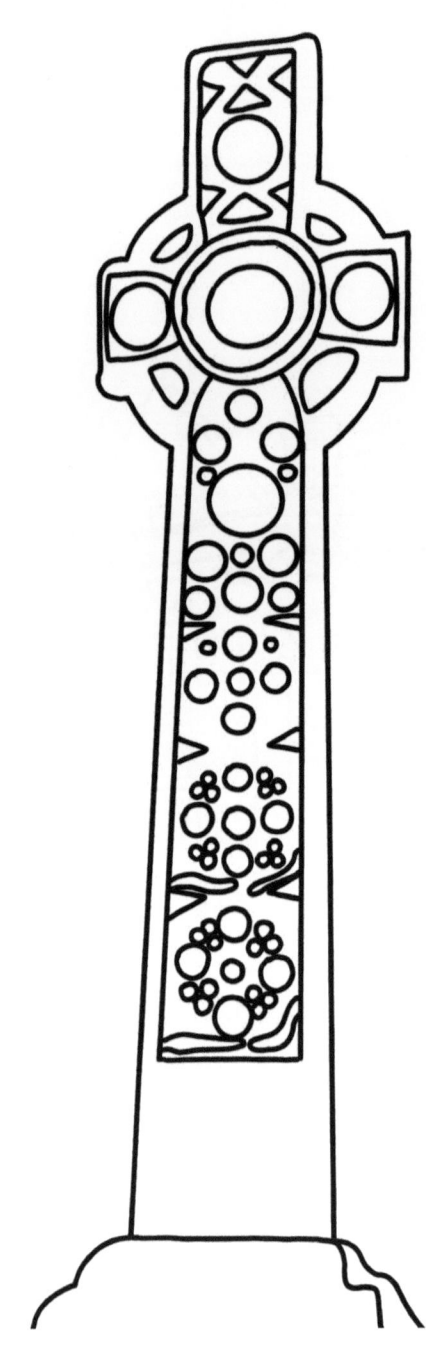

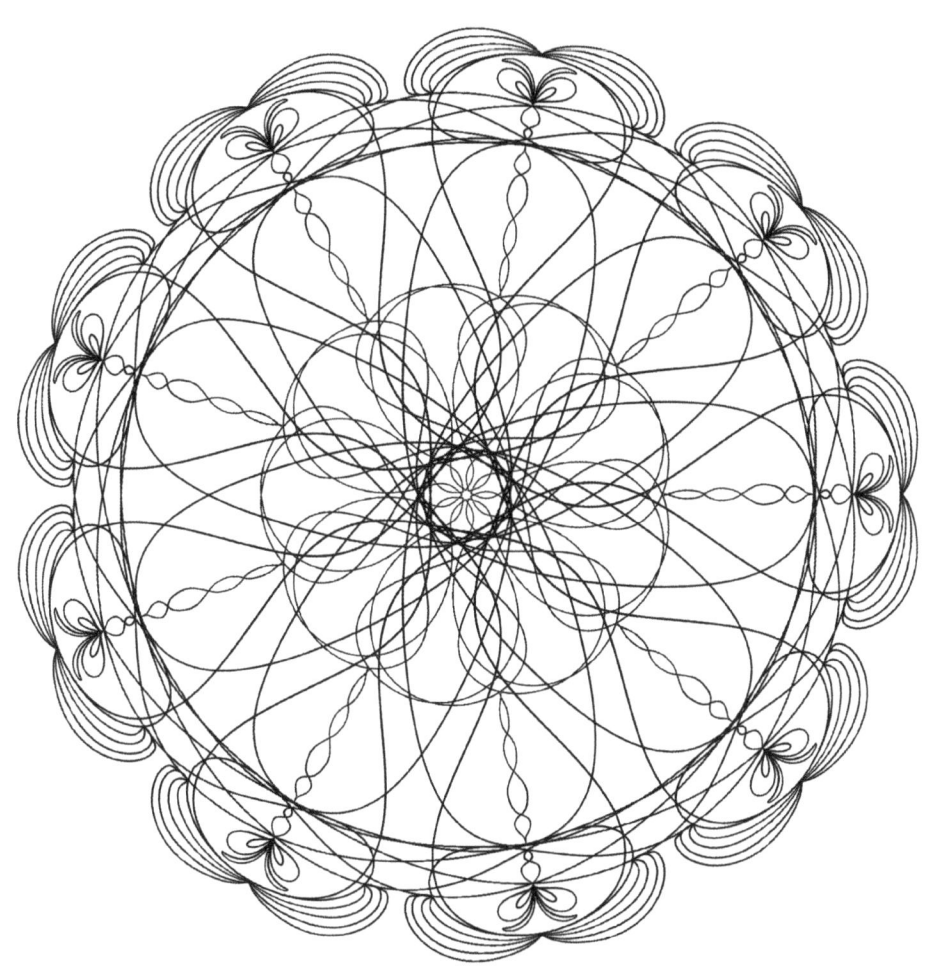

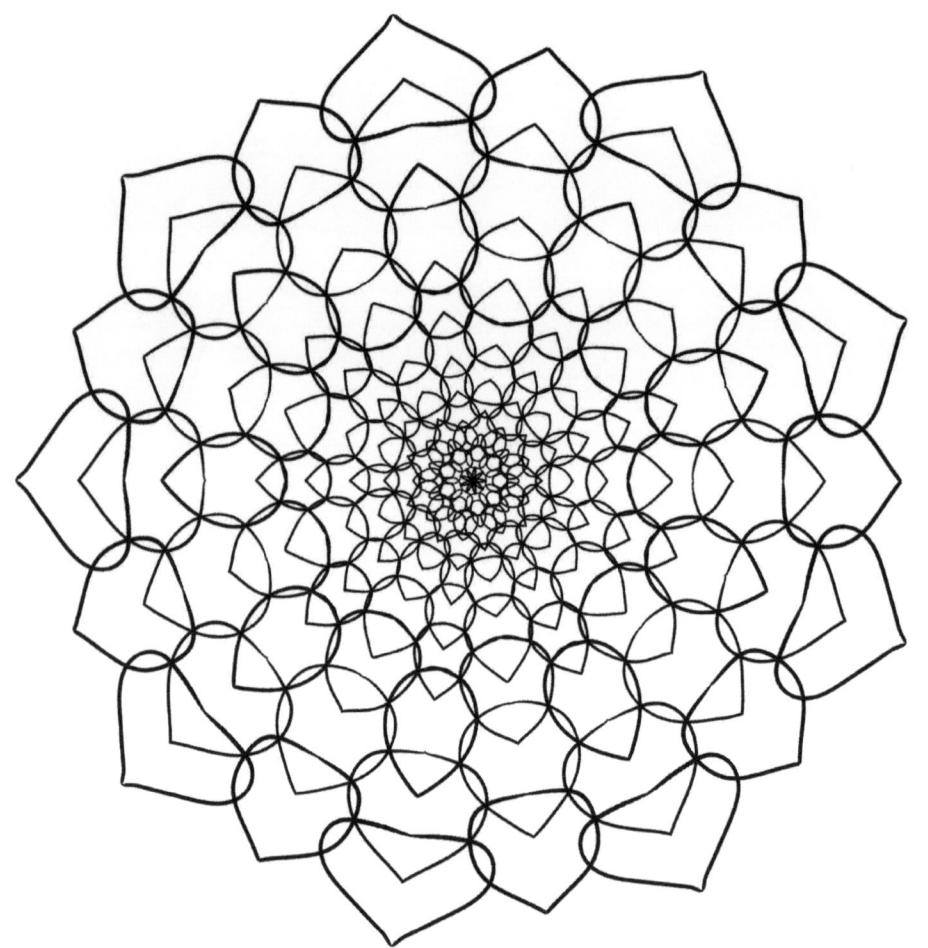

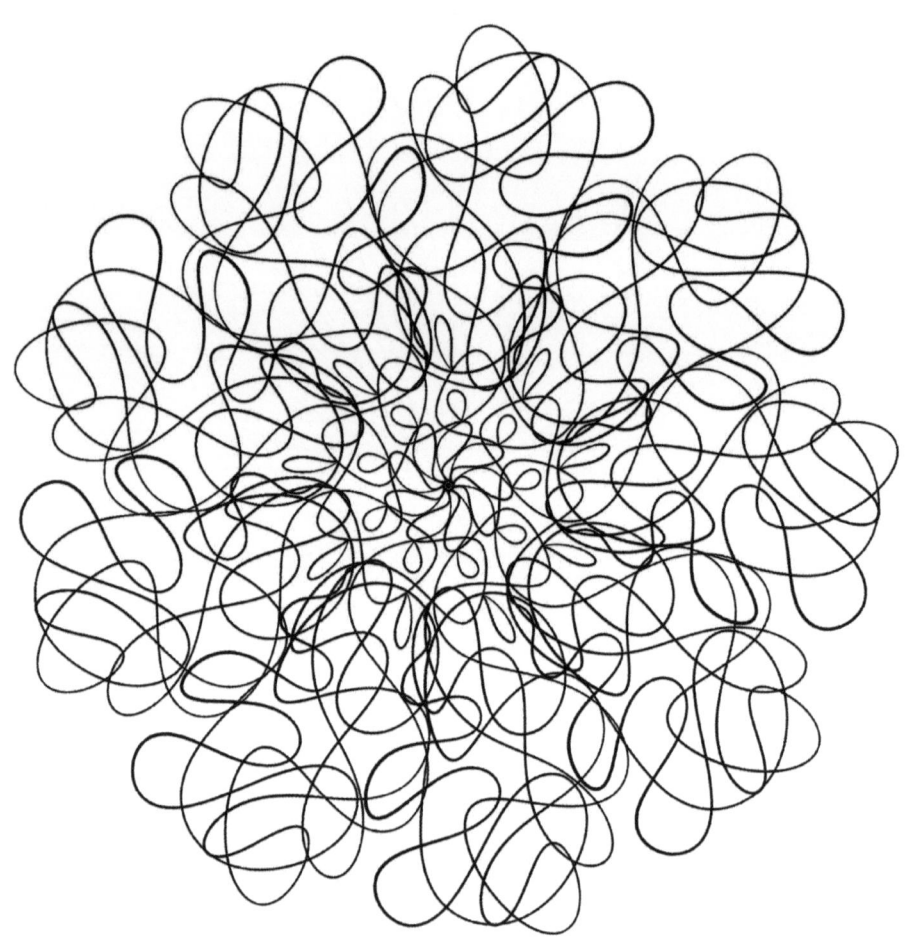

Emma Major is a mum, wife, friend, pioneer lay minister, blind wheelchair user, poet and artist. Her work was featured on the Channel 4 series *Grayson's Art Club*, and she is the author of *Little Guy: Journey of Hope* and *Caring for Creation Together* (Wild Goose Publications).

Wild Goose Publications, the publishing house of the Iona Community established in the Celtic Christian tradition of Saint Columba, produces books, e-books, CDs and digital downloads on:

- holistic spirituality
- social justice
- political, peace and environmental issues
- healing and wellbeing
- innovative approaches to worship
- song in worship, including the work of the Wild Goose Resource Group
- material for meditation and reflection

Visit our website at
www.ionabooks.com
for details of all our products and online sales